ULTIMATE TREEHOUSES

ULTIMATE TREEHOUSES

DAVID CLARK

COURAGE BOOKS

AN IMPRINT OF RUNNING PRESS
PHILADELPHIA • LONDON

2003 Salamander Books Ltd
Published by Salamander Books Ltd.
The Chrysalis Building, Bramley Road
London W10 6SP, United Kingdom

© Salamander Books Ltd. 2003
A member of **Chrysalis** Books plc

This edition published in the United States in 2003 by Courage Books, an imprint of
Running Press Book Publishers
125 South Twenty-second Street
Philadelphia, PA 19103-4399

9 8 7 6 5 4 3 2 1
Digit on the right indicates the number of this printing

Library of Congress Control Number: 2002116206

ISBN 0-7624-1638-6

Notice: The information contained in this book is true and complete to the best of our
knowledge. All recommendations are made without any guarantee on the part of the author or
publisher. The author and publisher disclaim all liability in connection with the use of this
information.

CREDITS

Commissioning editor: Marie Clayton
Designer: Cara Hamilton
Reproduction: Anorax Imaging Ltd
Printed and bound in China

This book may be ordered by mail from the publisher.
But try your bookstore first!

Visit us on the web!
www.runningpress.com

contents

a little bit of history

Right: The open gallery running round this modern treehouse at a lower level, overlooking the lake, is an ideal place to sit, enjoy a drink and admire the wonderful view.

Treehouses capture the imagination, and they appeal to the child within us all. They do not have to be just for children—they can be a retreat for adults, a place away from the phone where no one can reach them (be sure to leave the mobile behind, though!). They can be a play house, or a private place to read or paint, the venue for cocktails or tea— or even a working office or den if spare space in the home is short. Those of us who love nature value the way a treehouse takes you up to a birds' eye view of the world, up amongst the leaves with the squirrels and other arboreal animals. It is very difficult to be stressed in a treehouse. Anyone who has enjoyed relaxing in a hammock slung in a summer orchard, or sitting on a treehouse veranda—or on any platform up a tree—will confirm the uniquely satisfying qualities of peace, of detachment from the rat race below and of closeness to nature.

Being without man-made foundations, walls of stone or concrete, large hearths or any other very solid and long-lasting features, treehouses do not (yet) appear in the western archeological record. But this does not mean that they did not exist. Although we might not be able to find them now, treehouses must certainly have existed since time immemorial. Paleontologists are aware that before venturing onto the ground—to risk becoming prey to larger wild animals—Homo Sapiens lived in the trees and it is certainly possible that we only learned to walk as a means of getting to the next tree! However, remains of those very early treehouses—or indeed any other kind of dwelling place from that era—are lost to us forever, although a few stories of them have been passed down through the ages.

In the days of the Pharaohs, the trees growing in Egypt were surely host to the occasional treehouse where little Caesars could look out over Rome. The Emperor Caligula is certainly recorded to have held banquets in a treehouse built in an enormous plane tree. Columbus doubtless surveyed his family garden from an elevated vantage point up a tree, before growing up and setting out to seek much wider horizons from the crow's nest of the *Santa Maria*.

During the Italian Renaissance, the infamous Medici family built a small marble palace in a tree. The enlightened romantics of the eighteenth and nineteenth centuries enjoyed follies, including rustic

Below top: A hovel in Chelsea, engraving by J.T. Smith c.1800.

Below bottom: Hermitage for a gentleman's park from Jardins Anglo-Chinois, 1776.

cottages with trees growing out of them and trees with rustic hovels wrapped around them. They introduced an ambiguity between the tree-house and the house-tree that still persists to today. Often the hovels provided more comfortable accommodation than the real workers' cottages—for example, J.T. Smith published an engraving of a hovel in Chelsea, circa 1800, where the distinction between tree and house is very blurred. This compares unfavorably with "the hermitage for a gentleman's park" (from Le Rouge's Jardins Anglo-Chinois pattern book of picturesque follies of 1776)— which coincidentally shows the beginnings of a treehouse style that still survives today in Adahu Abaineh's house in Addis Ababa, which is described in Chapter Seven. In the mid-1900s, celebrated eateries in a town west of Paris had the diners seated on platforms high in the majestic trees, and their food was hoisted up to them. Robinsons was a popular rendezvous in Paris itself—diners could dance or promenade at ground level, before ascending into the tree tops to enjoy their meal. Unfortunately nothing now remains of these once elegant and unusual restaurants.

Although they may be very sturdy in themselves when new, for a treehouse to survive from long ago until the present day several coincidental conditions all have to be met:

• It must be in a tree that is sufficiently sturdy and long-lived to survive across many years, and one that grows and spreads only at a very gentle pace.

• The treehouse itself must be sufficiently loved to be cared for through the generations, and to receive basic maintenance or better.

• The environment must be sufficiently placid so that the tree and its structure does not succumb to forest fire, storms or hurricanes, to tsunami or floods—or even to drastic shortages of firewood in winter.

• The location needs to be in a fairly stable human environment—preferably not the scene of a major battle, or a world war, nor in an area likely to become swallowed up by factories or submerged under motorway routes.

Fortunately, a few places do exist where these eccentric coincidences are met and so rare examples do come down to us from long ago. Fairly well

Below: Robinsons in Paris, c.1905. Diners enjoyed their meal high up in the branches; their food was hoisted up to them in a wicker basket.

1. ROBINSON — Le Gros Châtaignier

11ᵇⁱˢ. ROBINSON — Le Vrai Arbre

Javelle, phot., Robinson

Left: Elevated dining for social climbers? One of the baskets used to hoist food up to the diners can clearly be seen in this contemporary postcard view. It looks like it was quite a climb to the top— but the view must have been worth it.

Above: Treehouse living is the norm for many people around the world—as here in the Philippines.

Below: Queen Elizabeth II revisits Treetops, where she first stayed as a young princess.

known is the treehouse at Pitchford Hall, Shropshire, the first generation of which dates back to 1692, thus giving it fair claim to be the oldest surviving example. Propped and balanced soundly in a broad-leaved lime tree, it underwent restyling in 1760 and modernization in the 1980s. The treehouse is built in the same half-timbered style as Pitchford Hall itself, with gothic windows on all sides and a part-glazed door that opens to reveal an interior with a carved molded cornice ceiling and an oak strip floor. The estate went into private ownership some time ago, so unfortunately the general public no longer has access to this wonderful architectural record.

Potentially older (although failing now under threat of destruction by modern man), must be the houses of some of the animist tribes of Northern India, which are set high in the branches. Similarly, the Kombai and the Korowai peoples of western Papua New Guinea have a culture of treehouse living that reaches far back into the mists of pre-colonial times. The Philippines also have tribes who live in treehouses. Undoubtedly such cultures once existed throughout the tropical forests, where small tribes lived detached from one another and in fine balance with all the products of nature.

Stretching the definition (although not the spirit), far older still are the nests of chimpanzees and orang-utans, which display all the fundamental features of modern treehouse building. Although they typically reduce walls, roof, doors

and windows—and access ladders—to an absolute minimum, they almost always feature some form of roof covering made simply by curving branches over the platform and securing them in place.

Older still, and straying further from the more obvious human connection, are the nests of birds. While not meeting many of the requisites for true treehouse status, the nests of some birds do meet the sheer size requirement (storks and some birds of prey for example) while others (magpies and wrens, for example) manage to create excellent roofs. Whether this can be used to hypothesise that the forerunners of Man learned treehouse building from *Archaeopteryx* and his relatives is for others to consider!

A more recent and well-known treehouse is Treetops, which is situated in the Aberdare National Park in Kenya. This was where the then Princess Elizabeth was staying in 1952 when her father, George VI died and she became Queen Elizabeth II of Great Britain overnight. In those days it was a very unusual and unique place to stay, but now there are treehouse hotels in several places in Africa, and in many other countries around the world, including America, Hawaii, India, China, Australia, Belize, several Caribbean islands and Thailand.

It is certainly true that people have made use of trees for refuge, observation, relaxation, shelter—and generally for just living in—just as long as the trees have been there. Modern man is only following on this established tradition—although some of the structures built today are so sophisticated and technically complex that we might well be accused of moving away from the natural world. These days some people have treehouses that really are a home from home—complete with wide screen television, sofas and and a décor that would be equally at home in a town house. Such structures may be houses in trees—but unless you are in touch with the rhythms of nature when you are inside, and can sense the movement of the branches in the breeze around you, I wonder whether such structures are really treehouses at heart.

Below: Treetops is the original tree lodge, and it is still in operation today. It overlooks a waterhole and has 50 bedrooms, four decks and a rooftop viewing platform.

treehouses in fiction

Below: This British advertisement for Kellogg's Corn Flakes, c.1960s, is based on an idyllic fantasy of a happy childhood up in the trees.

One of the delights of fiction is that it can stretch the boundaries of imagination and create new worlds that may not—or cannot—exist in the physical environment. Once the mundane laws of physics can be disregarded, the treehouse can reach a new complexity and become truly inspirational. Such structures might not be extant, but they do come down to us in literature. Treehouses in modern fiction and storytelling often has an association with fairies, elves, teddy bears or escapist families. Unfortunately this has resulted in a kind of accidental niche marketing, which tends to distract from the universal pleasure that is derived from sitting in trees!

A child's first introduction to the concept of the treehouse is likely to be Owl's House in 100 Aker Wood in *Winnie-the-Pooh*. In fact many of the characters in this book live in or around trees—including Winne-the-Pooh who lives under a tree, and Piglet, who lives in a "grand house" in the middle of a beech tree. In the original 1920s illustrations by E.H. Shepard, Christopher Robin himself has a front door that is set in a large tree trunk—although it apparently leads into a much bigger house, with a staircase and proper bathroom. It was only when the stories were animated by Disney that Christopher Robin began to live in an ordinary-looking house, at the edge of the wood.

Peter Pan and the Lost Boys lived on a tropical island, and in the many illustrations of the story made through the years they either live in the branches or in a trunk of a tree. In the Disney animated film their home was an underground cave, accessed through a tree, and in *Hook*, the 1991 film of the story starring Robin Williams, he and the lost boys lived in a kind of modern-day adventure playground, with rope ladders and a fort.

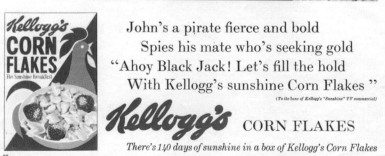

Kellogg's CORN FLAKES
The Sunshine Breakfast

John's a pirate fierce and bold
Spies his mate who's seeking gold
"Ahoy Black Jack! Let's fill the hold
With Kellogg's sunshine Corn Flakes "

(To the tune of Kellogg's "Sunshine" TV commercial)

Kellogg's CORN FLAKES

There's 140 days of sunshine in a box of Kellogg's Corn Flakes

Older children may remember the fantastic creation of the *Swiss Family Robinson*, who managed to build a veritable palace in the treetops with only a few items salvaged from the wreck of their ship. Most illustrations of this—both in books and films—show it as having several rooms and many floors, connected by platforms, rope bridges and ladders, with access that could be pulled up at night to avoid wild animals. (Although what they did about the wild animals that could climb the tree is never satisfactorily explained). This survivalist construction was built for practicality, but in so doing it manages to achieve a fictional elegance.

Another famous treehouse-dwelling character is Tarzan. Although he moves around the forest with the apes who reared him at first, things change when he meets Jane. In most visualizations of the story, both in books and on film, he then builds a sturdy and rustic treehouse, which is nevertheless filled with home comforts, for his beloved to

Below: Arwen, in her arboreal palace, as portrayed by Peter Gabriel in the 2001 film of *Lord of the Rings.*

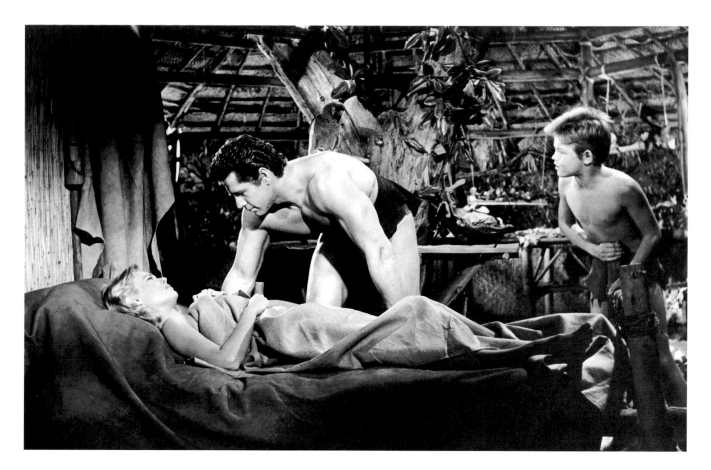

live in. No doubt she put her foot down firmly when he first suggested that they should just live in the branches like his other relatives!

Visualisations of Tolkien's *Lord of the Rings* typically show elfish dwellings to be galleried, leafy and elevated—even those of Rivendell, which in the original book are never described as set in trees. The palaces of the Lady Galadriel, high in the Mallorn trees of Lothlorien, are portrayed by Peter Gabriel as an arboreal Big Apple, with staircases lit by glow worms spiralling up to fantastical heights. And neither a nail nor a bolt in sight!

Meanwhile, Richard Marquand in *The Return of the Jedi* places the homes of the Ewok, the teddy bear folk of the moon of Endor, as a series of high-up dwellings forming an elevated utopian suburbia—treehouses for all classes. The Ewoks are technologically primitive, but they have built huts with thatched roofs and animal-skin curtain doors, linked with rope ladders, wooden catwalks and swinging vines. Treehouses and space seem to go together in a strange way—maybe it's something about being up in the sky—as there is also a treehouse village in *Flash Gordon*.

In the fairytale *The Baron in the Trees*, by Italo Calvino, a young nobleman spends his entire life in the branches of the trees surrounding his estate. This book was cited as a source of inspiration for those planning to enter the 2001 international competition to Design a Treehouse for a Tropical Island.

Above: Tarzan makes Jane comfortable in their treehouse, in *Tarzan's Fight For Life*, released in 1958 and starring Gordon Scott as Tarzan, Eve Brent as Jane and Rickie Soresen as Tartu, Tarzan's adopted son.

backyard buildings

It is surely every child's dream to have their own space hidden away from view—and even a secret wish for many adults too! Children normally live in the adult world, and have to adapt as best they can to their way of life, but in a treehouse children can have their own world that does not necessarily follow adult rules—in fact can even ignore them entirely! Even the most basic structure in a tree can become a castle in the sky, or a jungle lookout. If it is not possible for you to build your own, there are several professional companies that will create something just for you.

Wild Wood, a company in England, has been building treehouses for many years—mainly for children, but also some for adults as well. Phil Muil of Wild Wood builds treehouses that are individually designed to meet the requirements of those who will use them. He tries to get into the mind of a child—to see things from their point of view and to come up with a creation that they will enjoy for many years to come.

Wild Wood treehouses feature hidden corners, secret hideaways, lookouts and castles, all built in solid wood. A variety of different exits and entrances—some concealed behind furniture or other fittings—along with rope bridges, double rope walkways, slides and fireman's poles, give a child an exciting way of moving round the site in several ways without being seen, Each treehouse is different, because each is designed around the specific tree, to suit the client and to fit in with the quirks of the site.

Wild Wood also tries to make their treehouses fit into their environment and to have a natural and organic feel. The next few pages show a selection of Wild Wood projects, along with a brief description of each and some details of the design.

Below: An original concept design drawing for one of Wild Wood's treehouses.

lime tree platform

The ramp shown here in the foreground was specially installed to allow the owner's dog to get up onto the deck! It leads to a wide fork in a tree, through which you step onto the rope bridge—which runs across to another large tree on the other side of the garden. The rope bridge was constructed by hand on site, with the rope being threaded through the wooden floor slats. It has safety netting woven into the sides, so even the smallest child cannot fall through.

From the rope bridge, you step through another tree fork, onto a large platform between two lime trees. The platform had originally been planned to take a large treehouse, but unfortunately the construction was vetoed by local planning officers so it is now used as a massive drinks deck. From the platform, a fireman's pole takes you straight to the ground—or for the rather more agile and adventurous there is a knotted rope instead.

willow treehouse

The willow tree masking this treehouse was not strong enough to support it, so the structure is actually a self-supporting stilt house—which now supports the tree!

The access to the platform is hidden behind the tree, and the treehouse itself has a stable-door and custom-built, fully-opening windows. Everything is painted to harmonize with the surroundings. Inside the treehouse there is a secret trap door under a bunk bed, which gives access to a few steps leading under the platform.

Left: Next to the fence is a climbing wall, with a rope up to and down from the platform. The whole structure provides lots of different ways for the two young boys who own it to enjoy themselves.

Opposite and top: From the platform, there is also a double rope walkway that leads to a small tree nearby, from which there is a rope ladder down to the ground. Adults can use the wooden steps to the platform instead!

fairytale treehouse

In this fairytale treehouse designed for young children, all the walls twist and turn to give an idiosyncratic look. The cladding boards were chosen for their two-tone effect.

Since children like lots of different ways to move around, the treehouse has secret entrances, a slide, a fireman's pole, knotted ropes, a scramble net—and a castle at the end of a bridge leading away from the treehouse. The access staircase again twists round the tree, offering different views of the garden.

Opposite: From this angle, the treehouse blends into the tree and appears visually to be much smaller than it actually is.

Left: All of the fittings are specially designed and carved of wood on site—even the hook for the "essential supplies" basket.

Below: The treehouse has several entrances, while the bridge leads to a separate castle a few yards away.

conker castle

This attractive treehouse is built 10-12 feet up in a beautiful horsechestnut tree, in the garden of a house in Islington, London. It belongs to three agile girls who have christened it "Conker Castle"—as shown above on the sign they made themselves.

A rope ladder provides the only access to the platform—which the girls like as it keeps the adults out! For the very brave, there are also discreet steps on the outside beside the tree, which lead up onto the roof of the treehouse and a crows nest in the tree itself.

Left: The window shutters, with their neat heart-shaped cut outs, have a sturdy hand-made oak latch to keep them closed during wet and windy weather.

Opposite: The planking of the treehouse hugs the shape of the tree exactly, and the roof is double-skinned to make sure it is completely waterproof inside.

This treehouse was commissioned by a famous English actress for the garden of her home in Cornwall, and it was the first major project for British company Wild wood. Her brief was that it should look as if it had been built with materials salvaged from a wrecked ship, or found in the wood surrounding the proposed site. This is very appropriate for the setting, as you can look out over the Cornish sea from the deck.

The treehouse is built in a pine tree that has blown down, but is still living, so that the house sits in amongst its twisted branches. As well as the tree, the structure has additional support from old telegraph poles, which are dug into the ground and concreted in place. These still have some of their old fittings, such as triangular steps and ceramic cable holders. Parts of the treehouse are built from salvaged pieces from "Shiver Me Timbers," a reclamation yard in Penzance, Cornwall.

Wild wood always tries to find and build with the unique spirit of the tree, so the unusual spiral staircase that takes you up to the platform follows the shape of the curving branch.

ship's deck   tall treehouse ▶

This deck, built for children, is designed to feel like a ship riding the branches. The ropework railing gives a sense of rigging, there are hatch-like trapdoors that open up into the bowl of the tree and two masts for running up flags—as well as a wooden cannon that is not visible here. Access to the deck is via a spiral pole ladder, through a small hole in the deck floor. Since it is built on a site subject to quite high winds, the structure is designed with complex sliding joints to accommodate the movement of the tree. In a strong wind, the whole structure sways like a ship under sail.

Although this treehouse is only 60 feet from a busy road in North Oxford in England, it is completely hidden from passers by. It is set 13-14 feet above the ground, so the railings are designed to be very sturdy and safe with the cross rails on the outside so there is no purchase for climbing. Access to the platform is via a hidden series of platforms and stairs in the adjoining pine trees. When construction was begun the youngest child had just started walking, so the bottom rung of the first flight of stairs was left off to prevent him using the treehouse unsupervised!

beechwood treehouse

From one side this treehouse looks just like a log cabin, built in and set amongst beech trees. From the other, it has a castle keep, which can be accessed either from the platform or through a secret cupboard under the bed in the treehouse. A ladder leads up inside the tower to the top, which gives views across the whole site. The treehouse is completely waterproof and has lighting, so that the children can sleep over in it at night.

A bridge from the platform leads to a rope walkway, on which the children can travel through the trees all the way to the far platform without touching the ground! This is the only way to reach the smaller platform, but from it there are two ways down—a fireman's pole or a zip wire.

Opposite: The rustic style of this treehouse suits the site.

Top: The children are big fans of Harry Potter—note the broomstick left leaning against the right hand outside wall!

Right: In this view the castle keep can be seen more clearly, behind the log cabin. From the top are views over the site.

ewok village   oak house ▶

Initially this was one treehouse, in a maple tree, but the two boys who own it wanted another room to sleep in so an extension was added. This has two camp beads and is accessed through the first house. The doors are lockable from both inside and out, so the children feel safe to sleep there at night. Another exit leads to a wooden bridge, which runs across to a crows nest in another maple. The crows nest has a speaking tube connection to the main treehouse. From it, you can return to the ground via a fireman's pole, or climb across a double rope. Since the complex looks like something out of Star Wars, the two young owners have christened it "Ewok Village."

As this treehouse was built for very young children, it has an easy access ramp with a rope handrail leading to the first platform. From there, a short flight of stairs takes you up to the door of the treehouse, and inside another door leads to an upper platform, which is built round the tree. From the platform, a slide or a fireman's pole leads back down to the ground. The arched window has a small window box beneath it, so the children can plant flowering bulbs. To give the neighbors some privacy, a trellis to one side is planted with flowering honeysuckle. The roof has carved acorns as finials—and one is also included on the side facing the neighbors, so they have something interesting to look at!

a room with a view

Opposite: A general view through the forest of The Hideaway Treehouse, one of the four different treetop vacation rentals available at Treehouse Cottages, in Arkansas.

Below: Drawing of the Cedar Shade Treehouse from the brochure of Treehouse Cottages.

Most adults find treetop homes irresistible, and if self-build construction in your own backyard is not really for you, there are some wonderful treehouse hotels situated in different environments and in many countries all around the world. This kind of modern treetop living is in sturdily-constructed huts and usually comes complete with every convenience—including electricity, running water and sometimes even a telephone. It offers a way of living close to nature—while still enjoying many of the delights of civilization—that is very hard to beat.

There are a range of treehouse hotels and guest places, of different styles and offering different aspects of tree-living, from full-time to only sleeping in the trees. The following few pages can only show a small selection. One thing they do tend to have in common, though, is that they are usually set far away from mainline civilization—enjoy raw nature from your comfortable treetop room, and don't worry about the neighbors! Certainly being high up in the branches offers a different view of the world—fall asleep every night to the gentle swaying of the tree and wake up every morning to a wonderful view of the open sky and across the world beneath.

Many treehouse hotels make a virtue of necessity, and combine their offer of tree-living with ecological principles, trying to be self-contained and offering tourism with care for the local community. They use local materials and traditional techniques. Most also offer the local flora and fauna as attractions—either notes on what to look out for yourself, or organized tours—to make the most of your time living so close to nature.

treehouse cottages

Treehouse Cottages is a luxurious forest haven in Eureka Springs, Arkansas, with one romantic hillside cottage and three elegant treehouse cottages. Each of the treehouse buildings is more than 20 feet off the ground, supported on wooden poles. They were all created by the owners, Terry and Patsy Miller, with Terry—a talented builder and craftsman by trade—doing most of the building work himself.

Each of the cottages is a unique design, but they all feature arched doors, round stain glass portholes and picture windows, and are clad in natural cedar. The Hidden Oak Treehouse is 26 feet off the ground and has a great view of the valley below. Its heart-shaped jacuzzi sits in a bay window with glass on two sides. The Cedar Shade Treehouse is reached by a suspended bridge, over a cascading waterfall and goldfish pond. It is surrounded by forest trees, with its own deck and a romantic jacuzzi for two. The newest treehouse, The Hideaway, is deep in the woods and has splendid views over the surrounding forest.

Above: The Hideaway Treehouse is the latest building on the site. It is hidden in the woods, 22 feet up in the trees, with views over the surrounding countryside. The grounds of Treehouse Cottages are full of majestic trees, as well as flowers, a small pond and a waterfall. Although it looks as if it is far out in the country, it is actually within walking distance of the local town.

Opposite page above: The Hidden Oak Treehouse has a heart-shaped jacuzzi for two with a panoramic view, as well as a massive picture window.

Opposite page below: The hand-made log canopy bed, with a home-made quilt, in The Hideaway Treehouse. The cottage has a separate bathroom and a private outside deck.

tropical treehouse

Tropical Treehouse is a vacation rental in the lush tropical forests of the hills of Rincon', Puerto Rico. Jo Scheer and his family arrived on the island by boat, having sailed around most of the Caribbean islands and along the north coast of South America.

Here Jo became fascinated by bamboo as a construction material, making everything from lamps to complete bar interiors. In 1992 he discovered an abandoned sugar cane plantation and bought the land and buildings from the descendants of the old farmer. Over the next few years he worked the land, and planted some twenty species of bamboo—many of which have been utilized in the buildings seen here.

Above: View across the footbridge into the hooch (see pages 40-1) from the "mainland." The name "hooch" derives from a Japanese word meaning "shelter."

Opposite: Various views of the open balcony, with its relaxing hammock. Much of the building and its furniture has been designed and built out of local bamboo by Jo himself.

Bamboo has obvious aesthetic qualities, but it also has excellent compressive and tensile strength that make it a great building material. Its only drawback is its hollow nature, which creates difficulties in producing a strong joint. A rigid construction requires the use of proper triangulation, to relieve stress on the joints.

Another benefit of bamboo is that it has a very straight grain, so it splits predictably in a continuous line. Split bamboo can thus be easily used to make flexible screens and panels.

The main rental available at Tropical Treehouse is based around the original house on the site, to which Jo has added extensively in bamboo to create a wonderful airy building set within the trees—if not in them. The Hooch (see following pages) is an open-air bamboo gazebo, set over a change in ground level and supported by the surrounding trees. Jo has also designed and made much of the furniture, and the unusual bamboo light fittings.

Opposite: The master bed room, with its bamboo four-poster bed and chandelier.

Above left: The library/ office area has built-in bamboo shelving.

Left: Jo believes in creating designs that exploit the natural look and utilize the structural qualities of the material.

Below: Loo with a view? Open air living carried right through to its logical conclusion!

the hooch

The hooch is actually a room on stilts, rather than a treehouse, built over a drop in ground level. It is mainly built in local bamboo, with a translucent corrugated plastic roof—an interesting juxtaposition of traditional and more modern materials. The supporting poles converge to a single point at the base, with a footbridge to anchor the structure and tensioned cables to surrounding trees to maintain a perfect balance.

Below: A model of the pre-fab hooch, which is available from Jo Scheer in kit form.

Opposite: The original hooch, in Rincon', Puerto Rico, which has survived three hurricanes.

cedar creek treehouse

The large treehouse built by Bill Compher, near Mount Rainier National Park, sits 50 feet off the ground, halfway up a western red cedar. It is built of timber, but the tree is braced with a stainless steel cable. The access was originally via a 2x4 ladder, but Bill later added an enclosed staircase. The treehouse incorporates a living room, bathroom, kitchen and a sunroom/viewing room, with room for four to sleep in the loft. Solar panels power the electric lights, but water has to be hauled up via a pulley system. Bill lived in the treehouse himself for a couple of years, but it is now available for vacation rental.

daintree eco lodge

The Daintree Eco Lodge & Spa is a small family-run business designed to be "at one with nature." It is set in a beautiful location—one of the world 's oldest living rainforests, near World Heritage National Park in Northern Queensland, Australia. It is owned and operated by the Maloney family, who bought the project in its very early stages in 1995. The Maloneys formed their own environmental philosophy, which aims to provide a unique destination for the traveler whilst at the same time embodying the concepts of sustainable and profitable eco

and cultural tourism. They have also developed a close working relationship with the Ku Ku-Yalanji—the local Aboriginal community and original inhabitants of the area—to stimulate the local economy.

The elevated buildings—15 individual guest villas and the Bilngkumu restaurant—are perched on 30-40 feet up on stilts and set in a steep lush valley nestled in the rainforest. They are designed to protect the environment, being strategically positioned above the stream and beneath the rainforest canopy, which enables them to capitalize on the property's own cooler microclimate to reduce the use of electric fans and air conditioners. The elevated building design also limits human impact on the area, by ensuring there is little or no disturbance to the natural vegetation. Each villa has access to the restaurant via a system of elevated boardwalks through the rainforest. Essential services such as plumbing, power, water, and cabling are strapped underneath the boardwalks, again to minimize disturbance to the forest floor. The resort has its own natural waterfall in the grounds, which not only provides the total supply for guest use, but is also marketed as pure natural spring drinking water.

This is certainly not basic treehouse living. Each villa is luxuriously furnished and has an ensuite bathroom, telephone and tea and coffee making facilities. Some also have a private jacuzzi on the balcony, which is fitted with micro-screens to protect guests from insects. The resort is acclaimed as Australia's No.1 Rainforest Spa Resort and has won numerous tourism awards, including the British Airways "Tourism for Tomorrow" highly commended for Site &

Left: The 15 individual guest villas are set on tall stilts, which place them high up, just under the rainforest canopy.

Design, and two national awards for "Deluxe Accommodation" and "Ecotourism." It has also been listed as one of the top 4 spa retreats in the world. Guests are not only offered deluxe private accommodation, but also gourmet Australian cuisine, a health and relaxation spa, and a covered open-air swimming pool with adjacent sun deck. Those more interested in nature can enjoy authentic Aboriginal culture, personalized tours and activities, and an abundance of flora and fauna (some rare and endangered) to study and admire.

Despite its sense of exotic remoteness, the Daintree Eco Lodge and Spa is a 90-minute drive north from Cairns and only 45 minutes from Port Douglas, via one of Australia's top scenic drives.

Below: The villas are set overlooking the water, and each has its own private balcony—some of which have a private jacuzzi. The micro-climate of the site, and setting the villas beneath the rainforest canopy and next to the stream, reduces the need for air-conditioning.

Right: The interior of one the guest villas. Each of them is decorated in cool, pale colors, with natural marble floors and stylish bamboo furniture, to create luxury accommodation for 2-3 people. The windows and balcony are all fitted with micro-screens to keep any insects out.

fur & feathers

Situated in the southern Atherton Tablelands in the Cairns hinterland, Fur 'n' Feathers Rainforest Tree Houses is another Australian luxury eco-resort. The five treehouses here have been designed to have as low an impact as possible on the environment, and they blend into the surrounding trees. The area has never been cleared, so it still has its lush jungle, tall trees, vines, orchids and ferns.

The treehouses are built of timber and are perched on tall poles along the riverbank within the rainforest itself. Each has a large balcony veranda, with a gas barbecue and seating. The interiors are also finished in natural wood, and furnished with items made by local craftsmen. Many of the colorful fabrics have been printed using leaves from the forest, to create a unique feel to the interior.

Here, nature and civilization do seem to meet successfully. Each guest house is self-contained, with a fully equipped kitchen, living/dining area, bedrooms with king-sized beds, and a luxury bathroom complete with double hot tub. The kitchen even contains a dishwasher! But just so you realize you are in the rainforest, examples of the local wildlife—including possums, cat birds, parrots and the exotic fan-dancing Victoria's Rifle Bird—often come onto the verandas to join guests in the evening.

Left: The houses are set along the riverbank on tall poles, which take them up into the rainforest canopy. Each has its own large veranda—which overlooks the river—and comes equipped with its own fully-equipped kitchen, master bedroom, separate living room and double hot tub.

Below: The interior of one the guest houses. Each of them features warm, natural wood walls and floors, and stylish furniture, made by local craftsmen from indigenous timbers. The fabrics used in the interiors are printed using forest leaves. Each house sleeps from 2–9 guests.

big beach in the sky

In December 2000, Treehouses of Hawaii, in partnership with Sanya Nanshan Industry Dev. Ltd., opened four treehouses as vacation rentals on top and along a sand dune on the island of Hainan in the South China Sea. The treehouses are built high above the ground in beautiful old tamarind trees, with a fantastic view of the ocean, and within yards of a magnificent and seemingly never-ending virgin beach.

Building in this part of the world brings its own problems—the area is subject to typhoons and heavy monsoon rains, so structures have to be designed to cope with extremes of weather. David believes in using natural and locally-available materials, and in using traditional craftsmanship. He has also built other treehouses in Hawaii, and in 2001 launched a competition to design a treehouse, with the winning entries being built in Vietnam, China, Maui and Fiji (see pages 74-77).

Below: The interior of the treehouse features the living branches of the tamarind tree shooting up through the floor and out again through the roof. Open verandas offer a wonderful view of the white sand of the beach and the crystal clear waters of the South China Sea.

Right: View looking up into the structure of Big Beach in the Sky, which sleeps six comfortably on two levels and in a loft. It is set high in the branches of a tamarind tree, and is only accessible by suspension bridge. It is designed to withstand extremes of weather, such as typhoons and monsoons.

building your own
treehouse

Building your own treehouse is not only uniquely satisfying, if you do it with your children it can teach them how to use tools and how to work together in a team. Simple treehouses can be built with just a few basic techniques—which can be added to as required if you want to move on to a more complex structure. The design you work to will evolve naturally to some extent from the type of tree you have available and what you want to use the finished treehouse for. You will not need complicated tools—the equipment in the average tool box will probably be enough. Different fixings will be needed for different situations, so you will need a good selection of these. When purchasing lumber for your treehouse, choose pressure-treated, as it will last for 20–30 years. If you are using found materials, it is worth treating the wood with preservative yourself before you start.

The first thing to consider is where to build. In part this will be dictated by the position of available trees, but it is advisable to consider the privacy of your neighbors. Try not build right up against a shared boundary, or overlooking a neighbor's yard and, if possible, discuss your plans before you start. You do not necessarily have to take all their points on board, but if you can fit in with them to some extent it will be better for continuing good relations. Try to avoid building too near a road as well—you don't want to distract drivers and cause an accident.

TOOL HIRE

It is better to hire more expensive tools such as a compound saw (right) and larger masonry drills, than purchase them for an individual project. When hiring tools, especially power tools, make sure you receive all necessary guards, and a set of instructions or tuition from hire shop staff as to the correct way to use the equipment.

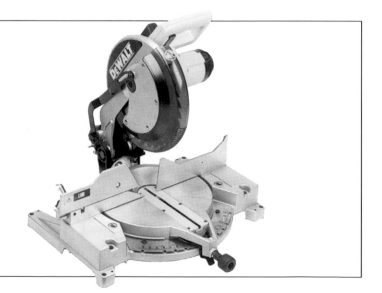

tools

Choosing the most appropriate tool for each job is essential. Using blunt or incorrect tools will slow down the work, leave a poor finish and could be dangerous.

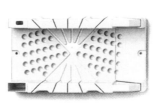

MITRE BLOCK

PENCIL SPANNER SHORT TAPE MEASURE LONG TAPE MEASURE

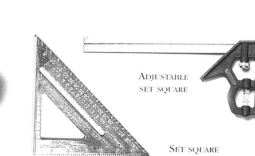

LONG SPIRIT LEVEL

SHORT SPIRIT LEVEL

FACE MASK

CIRCULAR SAW

ADJUSTABLE SET SQUARE

SET SQUARE

GOGGLES

SCREWDRIVER

SCREWDRIVER BIT

CORDLESS SCREWDRIVER/DRILL

CHISEL HAMMER BOLSTER HAMMER BOLSTER CHISEL

STRING

WOOD DRILL BIT

SAW

MASONRY DRILL BIT

tree varieties

There are many varieties of tree that are suitable to build in—and a few that are not. Deep-rooted trees such as Oak, Ash, Chestnut, Lime, Beech, Apple and Pear are better than shallower-rooted and more brittle types such as Elm, Sycamore, Cottonwood and Birch. Trees with spreading branches, such as Beech or Banyan, are suitable for single-tree structures, while those that grow tall and straight, like Lodgepole Pines, are better for constructions spanning several trees. Before making a final decision, consider the chosen tree itself. Is it strong enough to support what you plan to build? If you are using more than one tree, are they close enough together for your purpose?

DECIDUOUS TREES

Apple
A strong tree with a low, rounded shape and wide branches. Generally easy to climb, so a good choice for a children's treehouse.

Ash ▷
Has a straight trunk and an open crown and branches tend to grow in matching pairs, which makes it easy to plan a treehouse. Although it is tall it is also resilient, so it will flex in a strong wind. It provides excellent timber, but does have a tendency to drop its branches.

Aspen or Poplar
Fast growing and with a very short lifespan and weak wood.

Beech ▶

A very slow growing, tree, so structures will be safe for some years. The main branches of this tree spread wide, with lower ones sometimes pointing downwards. The nuts attract wildlife.

Birches

All varieties are too fast growing and with a very short lifespan.

Buckeye

Seed and young leaves are poisonous and the wood is too weak to support a reasonable structure.

Cottonwood

Fast growing tree and the wood is too soft to support any sizable structure.

Hickory

The wood of the Hickory is very hard, so it will be difficult to fix to. It also grows in an irregular way, making the design of a treehouse more difficult.

Maple ◀

Varieties of Maple grow in northern temperate regions. They have irregular branches and strong trunks. The Sugar Maple is the source of maple sugar and maple syrup.

Oak

A great tree for a treehouse— strong, easy to climb and with irregular but large branches. It offers a strong and firm support for a large platform.

Pecan
Again this tree has very hard wood, so it will be difficult to fix to.

Poison Sumac
The sap of this tree causes a skin rash.

Sweet Birch ▶
A tall strong tree with slender branches. Suitable for treehouses that spread across several trees, as long as they are growing close enough together.

Sweetgum
Best for supplying timber for the treehouse. It has quite open spaces between branches.

Western Red Alder
A short lifespan and rather brittle branches make this tree very unsuitable to take a treehouse.

CONIFERS & EVERGREENS

Cedar
Many species are commonly known as cedars, but the true variety is a slim tree that is similar to a pine but with wider branches that come down quite close to the ground.

Cypress
Closely related to the Cedar, but wider spreading. Not that suitable for a treehouse because of the number of closely-spaced branches.

Fir ◀
Several mature firs close together are perfect as living support posts for a treehouse, or a large fir can take a structure built surrounding the trunk.

Hemlock ▶

A graceful tree with relatively thin branches. Can be used to support a treehouse in a group, but older branches that drop downwards may need to be trimmed off.

Pine

Strong, straight and fast-growing, but some varieties have a limited number of branches so several in a group or additional support would be needed for a sizable treehouse.

Redwoods and Sequoias ▶ ▶

Very tall trees with drooping branches. Suitable for a treehouse very high off the ground—or the stump of a felled tree can make a great ready-made treehouse platform.

TROPICAL TREES

Banyan

A tree of warm climates and forms its own "forest" with its adventitious roots, which grow down from the branches into the earth to form pillars to support the tree. It grows very quickly and will intertwine with any structure, so a treehouse can end up being an integral part of the tree.

Bamboo

Not strictly a tree, but structurally very sound and ideal as support posts for a treehouse or house on stilts.

Pacific Madrone

Difficult to use as a treehouse base, but not impossible. A tree with very hard wood and often several trunks.

Palm

Several trees close together will be needed to support a large treehouse. Since Palms are flexible with no branches, fixings will have to be made direct to the trunk.

POINTS TO CONSIDER

• Check the tree itself and any nearby are healthy. You don't want to spend time and money only to find your tree is dying.

• Isolated sites will mean carrying equipment and materials a long way.

• Consider sleeping over on the site first, to check it out.

• Check out local laws—particularly if your treehouse is going to have power or plumbing!

• The design of the treehouse should evolve from the shape of the tree.

• Trees are flexible—so make sure your structure is too.

Left and above: The same basic shape of treehouse can look very different, depending on the design. These three cover much the same floor area, but just changing the style of the roof makes a big difference.

Some treehouse builders feel the best way to proceed is just to climb up and start attaching planks across branches, letting the structure evolve as you go. Although such constructions often have a certain charm, personally I feel it is better to have a clear idea of what you want to do before you start. It saves a lot of time and mistakes in the long run. When designing, you need to consider how best to fit your proposed structure to the tree. It is generally better to support the main load-bearing structure on branches, rather than fixing direct to the trunk. This not only gets wider as the tree keeps on growing (and a tight constriction round the trunk will literally strangle the tree) but branches are expendable and trunks are not. If the distribution of branches is not working out quite as needed, separate posts can be taken to the ground as an extra trunk (this device allows for much more flexible planning—there is no need for the trunk to rise in the middle, it can be at one end).

The type of tree (and the climate in which it is growing) will also affect the treehouse form. A slower growing hardwood—perhaps in the temperate regions where the wind is not so severe and the rainfall moderate—will allow a bulkier treehouse, sitting on the tree limbs with lots of headroom. A treehouse in a fast-growing tropical tree— perhaps bendy or prone to splitting, and tall and thin—will need to be tightly (but flexibly) tied in place. Comparison of the historic Robinsons treehouse on pages 8 & 9, with the hooch on page 37 illustrate how materials and environment can dictate form.

There are certain fundamental constraints to building a treehouse, but access is perhaps the most basic. Build at impossible height above the ground only if you need to—for effect, for observing, or to enjoy a spectacular view. For all other purposes it is best to establish a fine balance between being high enough to feel away from the ground, and being at a height that is inconvenient to reach or high enough to feel giddy. treehouses thus, unconsciously, tend to end up at similar heights—for children at around 5 feet up, for adult drinks decks 6 feet, for grown-up fun 12 feet, and for observing wildlife (and to keep out of reach of lions), more than 20 feet.

Trees do not heal wounds as we do. Instead they grow around them and carry on, so any wound made in constructing the treehouse should be kept to a minimum and treated like a cut on the arm—a little medicine and a lot of clean fresh air. It is more logical to drill or cut a branch (the treehouse design can be adjusted) rather than risk killing the tree by cutting the main trunk. Never cut into the bark all round the trunk—this is called ring barking and it will kill the tree very quickly.

Below: It is better to have a clear idea of what you want to do before you start. It saves a lot of time and mistakes in the long run. Detailed plans and elevations are not necessarily essential—a good sketch may work just as well.

platforms

The weight of the treehouse will bear onto large branches, perhaps supported from lower down the trunk with struts. A rough rule of thumb is to set the floor platform at one fifth of the total height of the tree. This means that the load is spread over a wide base area, wind movement of the trunk will have less impact, and the branches will help keep the floor in place. This floor platform becomes the base above which the walls rise and the roof is carried. It must be snugly supported rather than rigidly fixed—the latter will accentuate movement in the tree while a snug fit will minimise any swaying motion. Even those tropical treehouses, perched atop impossible slender trunks, are lashed tight to move with the tree. A point to note here is that the screws and bolts that lock any rope lashing should, wherever possible, be fixed in the treehouse lumber and not the tree branch.

Opposite: The supporting joists for the floor should be spaced a maximum of 24 inches apart. Lash the structure firmly to the tree. If branches don't fall where you need them, use a brace running back to the main truck to support the structure.

Below: The platform for one of Treehouse Cottages' buildings under construction in Arkansas (see pages 33-5).

Left: Protect the tree with pads, so the structure will not not rub away the bark as it moves in the wind.

An alternative method of construction is to brace out from the main trunk to support the floor beams. This is often necessary when building in Firs and Pines, where large branches to support the structure might not be available. The floor platform then forms a plate holding the tops of the braces together, and the trunk prevents it all from moving around. This method relies on a strong—usually bolted—connection of the brace to the trunk. With this approach, the trunk will pass up through the middle of the treehouse as the centre of gravity must be kept central, to pass the weight of the structure straight down the trunk. Take this into account when creating your design.

It is better to drill vertically through the tree limb rather than horizontally, as the latter will inevitably collect rubbish over time and the tree needs horizontal integrity to resist vertical loads. Cutting large sections of bark away to make drilling easier is to be avoided—only cut the tree when and where you absolutely have to; cut just enough to pass the bolt and the washer.

Because it is often very difficult to make the treehouse completely waterproof, it is a good idea to build the floor platform very slightly sloping away from the tree trunk. This is especially sensible if the treehouse is to incorporate an open veranda. It is also a good idea to build in ventilation, with slender gaps at the bottom of the wall and at the eaves, or floorboards spaced as they are on a deck, which will allow any damp to escape.

The platform is the most important part of the treehouse as it is the base for the whole structure, so take some time to be sure it is firm and level before proceeding any further. You should also bear in mind that trees are living organisms that grow and move in the wind, so allow room in fixings and make joints as flexible as possible.

Opposite: A treehouse platform high above the ground, with a spiral staircase under construction by Wild Wood, to provide access. As well as bracing, this example also has supporting posts, which form part of the stairs.

Below: Decking boards make a good floor, nailed firmly to the joists. Make sure the floor is level before going any further.

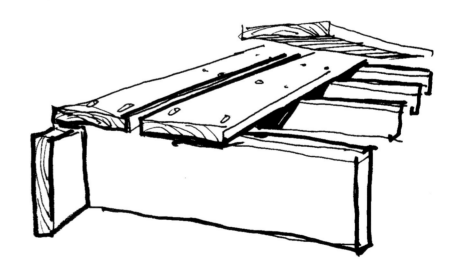

walls

Once you have a strong, sturdy platform in place, the rest of the construction is fairly easy. The walls add stiffness, carry the roof, keep the weather out and give the occupants privacy. The jointing should be tight but not rigid—timber is by nature flexible—and the panelling made accurately to fit, because a good fit will help to brace the whole structure, helping to keep it weatherproof and sound. Walls are normally in timber—although it is not absolutely necessary. In Renaissance times, the Medici treehouse was marble-clad, but then it was rather heavy and fell down. Insulation in the walls between the studs will extend the period in which the treehouse can be used. Although you might not intend to sleep in it, insulation will make it feel more comfortable in the heat of the midday sun and the cool of the evening. The external wall finish can be almost anything waterproof and weathertight—from the wattle and daub of Pitchford Hall, to woven mats of the Korowai people, to lap boarding or split lumber, to sophisticated sandwich panelling. It all comes down to personal taste—and fitting in with the look of the local neighborhood.

Opposite: Walls will need a framework to support the windows, doors and cladding. Framing is usually constructed of ordinary treated timber.

Left: Different types of cladding can be applied to the framework to complete the walls, depending on the style of building. Here, split logs have been used by Wild Wood for a rustic effect.

Inset below: If access is to be through the floor a trapdoor will be needed, both for privacy and to avoid an unsafe open hole.

windows & doors

Windows and doors are built just as in a typical house. Make sure the opening is square before fixing anything into it. Windows should be fitted with Plexiglass or left blank—glass is not a good idea as it breaks too easily. Putting

y.

over

arding

a cosy

heet steel

treehouses)

look. Beware

ehouse is in a

Below: Opening windows do not need to contain glass—if they do it should be safety glass—they can also have wooden shutters. This will make the interior dark when they are closed, but does offer more security when the treehouse is empty.

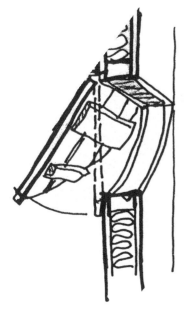

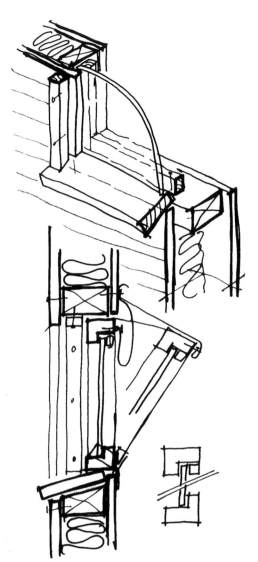

Above left: The door can be any shape, but the hinges must be placed vertically above one another for it to open and shut effectively.

Left: Here the door has been shaped along the top to follow the line of the roof. In the background, the door into the fort has a pointed Gothic-style top.

access

Access to your treehouse can be by steps, rope ladder, ramp or by climbing the tree. Small children will find proper stairs easier to climb, while for older children and (active) adults you can be a bit more adventurous. Once you have your structure in place, you can also add extras, such as a swing, slide or a rope walkway.

Above: Most children will enjoy a rope ladder, but adults may find them too much of an effort to climb!

Opposite, left and below:
A selection of different ideas for access ladders. The style chosen will very much depend on the age and fitness of those using the treehouse, and on the style of the structure itself.

railings

If the treehouse has a platform or a verandah, you will also need a railing of some kind for safety. If you are planning something exceptional—an open air hot tub, full-equipped kitchen, high tech recording studio—it is probably better to call in the experts. Equipment like this can be very heavy and installing it may also contravene local regulations.

Opposite: A simple but effective railing to a treehouse deck, made of closely-spaced posts. Note the cross bars are set on the outside, to discourage children from climbing up.

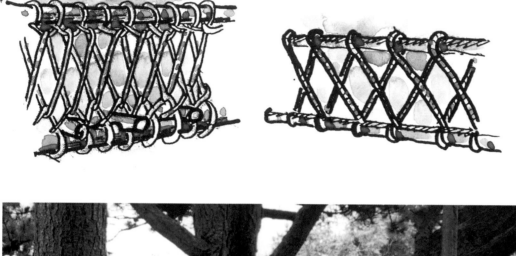

Left and above left: Rope wound round the upper and lower bars of the balustrade makes a decorative and safe barrier. Patterns can be quite simple, or far more complex, depending on how much time and effort is taken.

Above: Shingles or weatherboarding create a solid covering, providing privacy and safety, but perhaps restricting the view.

Right and above right: A more traditional railing, constructed from wooden posts glued and screwed together. Try out different designs on paper first.

CHAPTER 6

into the future

Below: Adahu Abaineh uses four trees—one at each corner—as the main load-bearing elements of his house, and then creates a frame between them with untreated wood poles. The walls are filled with traditional lightweight wattle and daub.

So where do we go from here? Rather than trying to build bigger and better versions of what we already have, maybe it is time to think laterally. An old trick of experienced gardeners is to plant a ring of fast-growing plants and allow them to shoot up and interlace, to create a living shelter—an arbor. It might be created by training roses over an artificial support, or it might consist of slender and flexible willow wands that can be bent and trained into shape. Some of these structures reached impressive stature during Queen Victoria's time—but they were playthings, not houses. But they could be houses… tree houses.

The distinction between tree and house is further blurred by the slowly developing "Tree House" living sculpture of Dan Ladd, as his apple trees are slowly trained into shape, and by Ewan McEwen and Clare Wilks as their willows grow up to form—albeit less architectural—a living tree house. Neither of these is intended to be a serious competitor to the room-up-a-tree version, but they do illustrate the breadth of thinking on the subject.

The relationship between man and trees in sub-Saharan Africa in the past has been very much one way—the trees have been slowly wiped out and the desert has advanced. Perhaps as a pointer to a new way, and perhaps as a subtle shift towards tree-lined avenues in place of primitive slums, architect Adahu Abaineh has created a truly inspired tree house in the suburbs of Addis Ababa in Ethiopia. His concept is simple, to use four trees—one at each corner—as the main load-bearing elements of his house, and then create a simple frame between them with untreated wood poles and fill in the walls with traditional lightweight wattle and daub (mud over interlaced twigs and small branches). The only factory-made material used is corrugated iron sheeting for the roof, which protects the fragile walls and channels rain to water the trees. His house took six weeks to erect and, despite initially treating the project with scepticism, his neighbors are now queuing up to learn his techniques. Such houses can grow with the family and the strategy can contribute to significant reduction in consumption of expensive manufactured building materials. Already groves of zigba and wanza trees have been planted nearby to be ready for houses for the grandchildren (and for the most patient of the neighbors maybe?).

Those log cabins that we see in heritage centers and in old Western films are the result of a long—and ultimately wasteful—process. The builder must find several trees, chop them all down, cart them to the building site and carve them carefully to fit together. He must lift and haul them, one on top of the other, and pin or peg them together until the walls are completed; then the roof timbers are propped on top and themselves braced together with yet more carefully-tailored pieces. Finally the whole lot is plugged, plastered and covered in. In the process, many trees are killed and much energy is expended to assemble a heap of carefully arranged firewood. And we call it a house. Maybe someday trees may be modified to produce a treehouse that we would be unable to recognize. Some day perhaps we will just grow one—plant the seeds for a three-bedroom detached chalet-style, that with only a little careful pruning will become a comfortable home

for our grandchildren, complete with growing roof and seasonal fruits. Only when it finally dies will we chop it up to provide furniture to go into the next home. Mr. Abaineh has created a solution that eliminates so many stages in the process of obtaining shelter and has, in doing so, reduced the scale of dependence on special equipment (saws, axes, adzes) and on transportation of heavy materials.

In a more technologically and artistically sophisticated context, the Dutch artist Dré Wapenaar has created his tree tents—gigantic green fruit that hang from a trunk like alien seed pods. They were inspired by the activity of anti-road protesters: "I wanted to offer them a relatively more comfortable stay in the trees during their protest actions. At the same time it is harder to bring down a tree when a tent is hanging on it." The fundamental form of the tree tent is that of a circular platform hanging by a rope from a tree

Above and below:
The tree tents created by Dré Wapenaar are like giant fruit that hang in the trees. The floor can be leveled by adjusting the two lower supports. They were originally designed to provide more comfortable accommodation for anti-road protesters, but now are situated in the Garderen campsite in the Netherlands

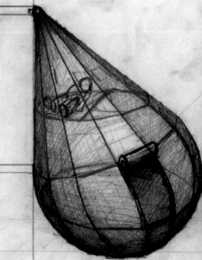

trunk. The avocado-green bag hangs from the top, at which point a nylon belt grips the tree trunk. The two lower support points are only to push the base away from the trunk, and are adjustable to enable the floor to be set horizontal. This technically elegant fruit would perhaps look as good growing from a street light pole, as from a tree. However, the future of the tree tent is in doubt as the only examples have been sold and now grace the Garderen campsite in the Netherlands. Its potential has not yet been fully developed—it has obvious application as a bird-watching hide or as guest accommodation, but perhaps it could also be used to provide fast and economical off-the-ground shelter.

The protest movement that inspired Dré Wapenaar has itself developed several tree house techniques—to create tree houses that are more intricate, interwoven and ever more difficult to remove. Often they are interconnected by rope bridges that are sometimes integral to the treehouse structure. They are designed as structures that are defendable; grown up versions of the forts and castles of childhood.

Until now we have dealt with relatively simple and straightforward arrangements driven entirely by resistance to gravity by means of props, posts and raking struts, of bolting to the tree trunk or of choosing large limbs to rest upon. Now we can begin to look at other ways of supporting a structure in a tree—by hanging it, by squeezing it, by bracing it with spokes of umbrellas and bicycles or by slinging it between two (or more) trees.

Developing from the tree tent might be an inflatable tree house, which would cling to the tree trunk as the wall and floor balloons were pumped up to high pressure. It would be squeezed into a secure position as it inflated, like a bouncy castle in the tree. A sheet floor could be added to further brace the structure and provide a solid base. This offers a method of creating a tree house with no bolting or drilling, which may be removed and taken on to the next tree or post—or even become the next house. A variation of the mobile home, perhaps! It could be independent of fixed services, inflated by a pump powered from a car, and with heat and light from storage batteries or by stringing the tree branches to take power from the movement caused by the wind. In areas prone to flooding it could float away if needed. It would need to be adjustable, or come in a range of sizes to fit a range of trees,

Below: The environmental protest movement often uses treehouses—both as a place to live and to prevent trees from being felled to make way for yet more roads. Usually built from *objets trouvé,* they develop on site to fit the tree and according to the materials available.

SUGGESTION FOR AN INFLATABLE
TREE HOUSE — SIMILAR TO THE
BOUNCY CASTLE IDEA — INFLATING
SO THAT IT FIXES IT TO THE TREE

rather than be tailored and fixed to a single tree—and it will not be suitable for prickly or spiny trees!

The International Treehouse Competition held in 2001 by David Greenberg sought new solutions to tree houses that were cyclone proof and buildable. The winning schemes are in process of being realized in developments in Vietnam, South China and Fiji.

Kendel Architekten produced an elegant design requiring at least two trees—the tree bivouac is suspended between the trees by creating a tensioned platform, on which the lightweight canopy of the tree house is constructed. While perfectly safe, the swaying and undulating as the breeze rustles the palm fronds will be very restful to hardy sailors and alpinists. Quite what it will be like for a holidaying young family awaits the construction of the prototype.

Above: Sketch design for an inflatable treehouse. It would cling to the tree trunk as the wall and floor balloons were pumped up to high pressure, and would be squeezed into a secure position as it inflated, like a bouncy castle in the tree. It certainly would not be suitable for prickly or spiny trees!

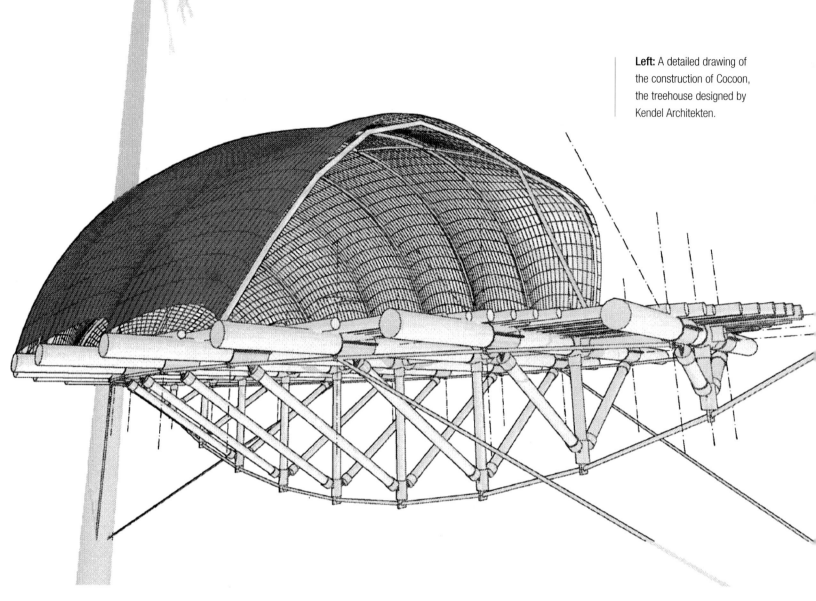

Left: A detailed drawing of the construction of Cocoon, the treehouse designed by Kendel Architekten.

Right: An artist's impression shows how Cocoon will sit between two palm trees, rather like a giant, upside down hammock.

Architects Marianne Bär, Jens Kolb and Peter Dör based their Coconut design on what the four Pacific beaches specified in the competition had in common—coconut palm trees and an ever-present breeze. Their treehouse hangs below the leaves of the tree like an out-size coconut, but it is made of high-tech materials such as light metal, carbon and acrylic. The outer shell of the coconut is of metal mesh, and it is suspended on elastic ropes between the palms, so that it is gently rocked in the ocean breeze. The modular system can be expanded both horizontally and vertically using suspension bridges.

The competition entry by Markus Bach uses bamboo as a construction material because it is cost effective, easy to work with and environmentally friendly. His design is based on geometric curved shapes, which can bear a higher load than straight elements. Four coconut palm trees support a structure system of four arches, which span 36 feet. Only one point is connected to a tree—the other three are flexible horizontally. The bamboo canes are joined using ropes and cords of bamboo rind or coconut palm fibers. Split bamboo is also used to make the screens and walls that clad and

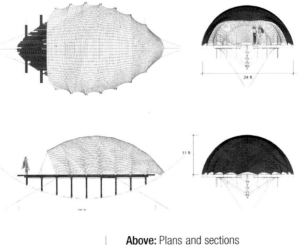

Above: Plans and sections show the construction. The structure uses locally-available wood, two palm trees, three different metal joints and a few meters of stainless steel cable.

Below: Artist's impression of the Coconut design, in situ on a tropical beach. The elasticated ropes hold the treehouse in a bungee suspension that gently rocks to the ocean breeze.

divide the space, so the entire project can be constructed in natural materials and using traditional techniques.

Looking further forward, tree house development is an area where genetic modification can be taken to logical conclusions. Vegetable life on earth thrives on our (animal) wastes: water— compost and carbon dioxide—while we thrive on the products of the plants around us—fruit, wood

Right: A section through Coconut, by Marianne Bär, Peter Dör and Jens Kolb. The pulley-operated basket is used for access.

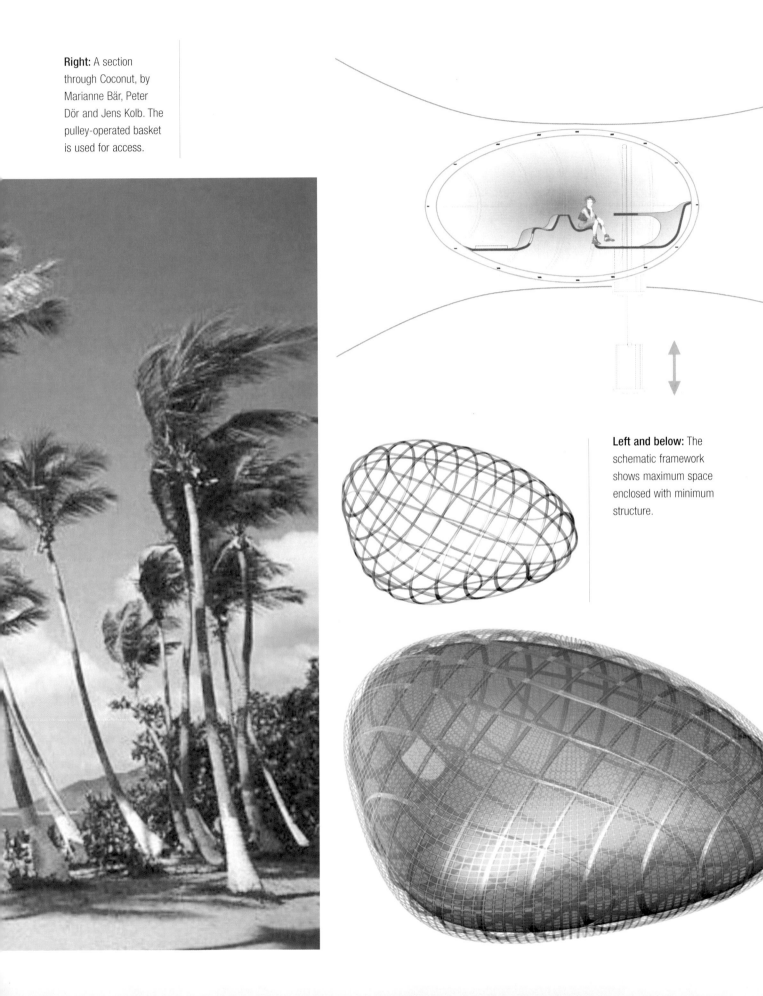

Left and below: The schematic framework shows maximum space enclosed with minimum structure.

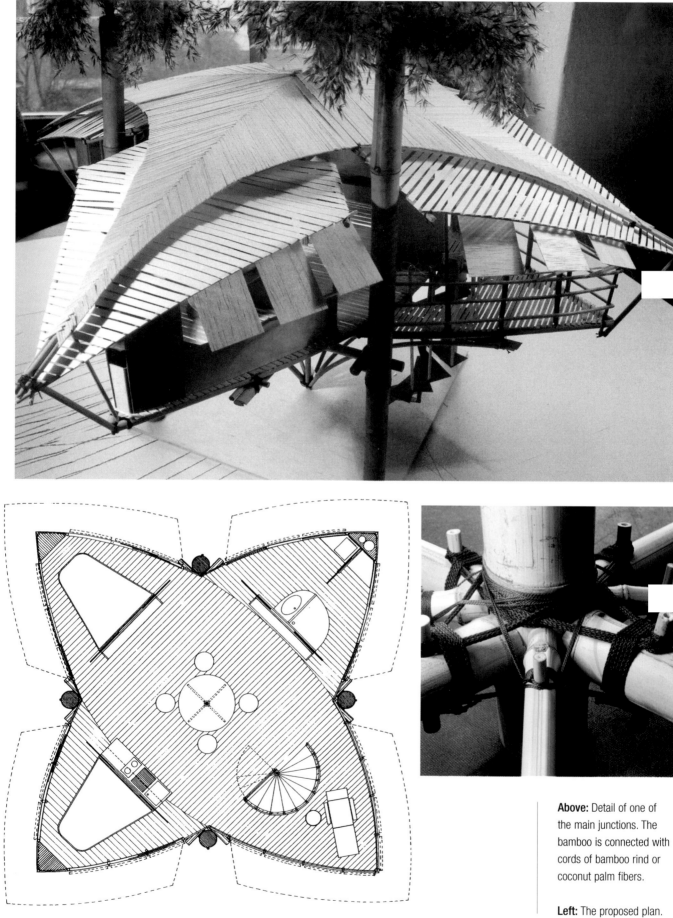

Above: Detail of one of the main junctions. The bamboo is connected with cords of bamboo rind or coconut palm fibers.

Left: The proposed plan.

Opposite: An architect's model of Markus Bach's treehouse design, showing its elegant form and structure. The open walls allow natural ventilation and the curved roof allows the structure to shed water easily.

Right: A section through the main area. The plan allows for separate sleeping areas, a bathroom, terrace and a large communal area in the center.

Below: View from below the model, looking up at the structure of the supporting platform.

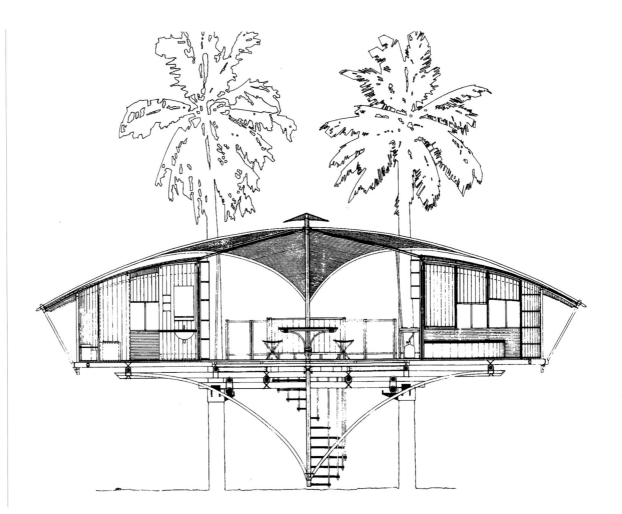

Above: A tree could be genetically engineered to grow to around 15 feet in height and then, by its natural process of growth, form a platform with fast growing straight branches at the edges—branches that could easily form the skeleton of walls.

and oxygen. It is obvious that the closer these two can be brought together the better, and as long as there is a balance of numbers between each, a mutually useful relationship could develop. The green revolution that we are living through has so far focused only on food crops—ever greater yields of wheat or rice—but it is not only these plants that can be studied. We are beginning to look at medicinal crops, crops that can take up and hold toxic chemicals and so clean up the environment... and next, crops that can be directed to grow in a shape or pattern to provide us with shelter—living tree houses?

Members of an older generation may be able to remember the technique of "pollarding" trees—cutting the lead branch out to leave a thick trunk topped with thin branches. These, fed by the deep root system of a mature tree, grew very fast and straight and were good for many uses. Imagine now a tree genetically engineered to grow to 15 feet in height and then, by its natural process of growth, form a platform with fast growing straight branches at the edges—branches that could easily form the skeleton of walls. It could be high enough from the ground to reduce shading, to allow plants—lawn, vegetables or just flowers—to grow close beneath, while not being too far to climb. The water from the shower or the kitchen sink could feed the tree and the plants—and they in turn could provide oxygen and sweet scent. The tops of the branches could shade the veranda in summer and be a windbreak throughout the year. Fantasy? Perhaps not—remember the mouse that was engineered to grow human ears?

Maybe this is also where we can think about the colonisation of other planets. For instance, Mars has a range of temperatures close to those of a Siberian winter, so perhaps a modified conifer—maybe crossed with a baobob for water preservation—could be developed to grow there. slowly, slowly adding oxygen to the thin Martian atmosphere. It would need a careful underground drip irrigation system—and maybe some protection from the ultra-violet radiation, but a Martian woodland would be a sight to behold. Of course a tree house on Mars will have to wait for another book...

Below left: A treehouse on Mars would certainly be a sight to behold!

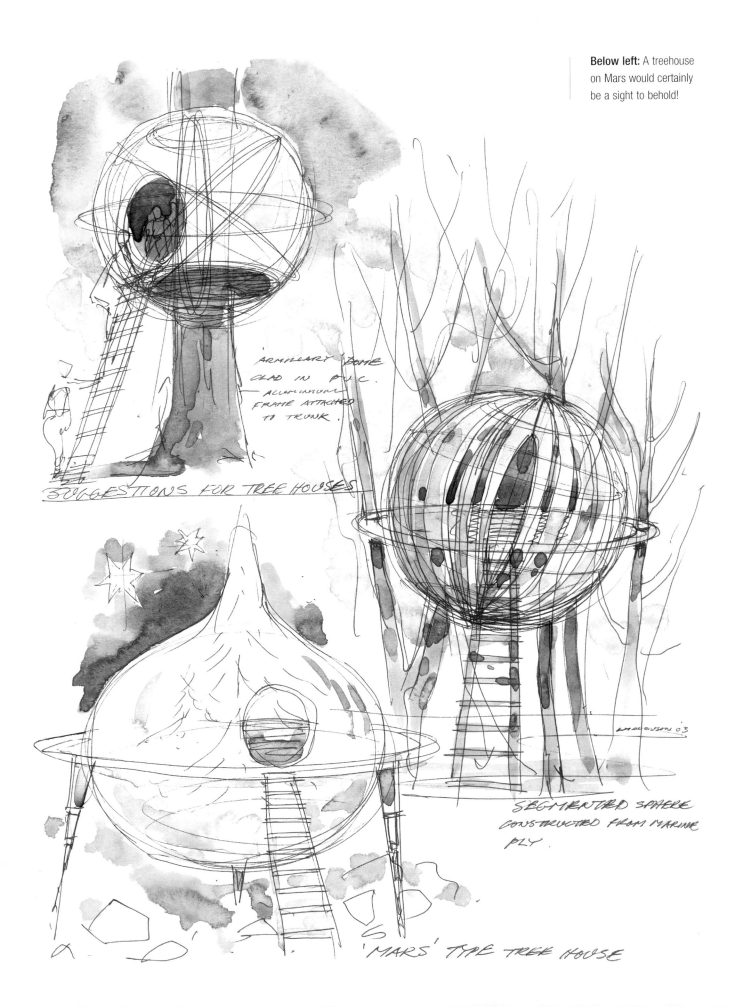

ARMILLARY DOME CLAD IN PVC. ALUMINIUM FRAME ATTACHED TO TRUNK.

SUGGESTIONS FOR TREE HOUSES

SEGMENTED SPHERE CONSTRUCTED FROM MARINE PLY.

'MARS' TYPE TREE HOUSE

picture credits

All images © **Chrysalis Images,**
except for the following:

Adahu Abaineh
P.O. Box3909
Addis Abbaba
ETHIOPIA
Tel: +25 19 21 54 38
Page 68

Advertising Archive
Pages 12, 13

Markus Bach
Schwedter Strasse 230
10435 Berlin
GERMANY
Tel/Fax: +49 30 4495787
Email: mb@wookee.de
Pages 76-7

Marriane Bär
Im Speicher 18
79353 Bahlingen
GERMANY
Tel: +49 7663 2647
marianne_baer@web.de
Peter Dörr
Werderstrasse 18
76137 Karlsruhe
GERMANY
Tel: +49 7213 70463
Pjdr@gmx.de
Jens Kolb
Collinistrasse 5
68723 Schwetzingen
GERMANY
Tel: +49 6202 14885
jens_kolb@web.de
Page 4, 74-5

Bill Compher
Cedar Creek Treehouse
P.O. Box 204
Ashford
WA98304
USA
Tel: +1 360 569 2991
Email: treehouse@mashell.com
Pages 42-3

Corbis Images
Pages 6, 10, 11, 70

Daintree Eco Lodge & Spa
20 Daintree Road
Daintree
Queensland   4873
AUSTRALIA
Phone: +61 7 4098 6100
Fax: +61 7 4098 6200
Email: info@daintree-ecolodge.com.au
Pages 44-5

Mary Evans Picture Library
Pages 8, 9

Fur & Feathers Rainforest Treehouses
Hogan Road
Tarzali 4885
North Queensland
AUSTRALIA
Tel +617 4096 5364
Fax: +617 4096 5364
Email: stay@.rainforesttreehouses.com.au
Page 46

David Greenwood
Tel: +1 808 248 7241
E-mail hanatreehouse@yahoo.com
Big Beach in the Sky
Sanya Nanshan Treehouse Resort
& Beach Club
Hainan
CHINA
Tel +86 1380 7500 909
Email: chinatreehouses@yahoo.com
Page 47

Kendel Architekten
Lindenallee 32
D-14050 Berlin
GERMANY
Tel: +49 30 301 6123
Fax: +49 30 30 61 43 62
www.kendelarchitekten.de
Pages 72-3

Kobal Collection
Pages 14, 15

Treehouse Cottages
165 W. Van Buren
Eureka Springs
Arkansas 72632
USA
Tel: +1 479 253 8667
E-mail: info@treehousecottages.com
www.treehousecottages.com
Pages 32-5, 56

Island Ambiance
Jo Scheer
459 Normal Avenue
Ashland
OR 97520
USA
+1 541 482 6357
Email bamboo@tropical-treehouse.com
www.tropical-treehouse.com
Pages 2, 36-41

Dré Wapenaar (designer)
vaandrigstraat 10
3034 px rotterdam
Studio: Tel/Fax: +31 10 2134346
Tel: +31 6 53438394
 Robbert Roos (photographer)
Singel 140
1015 AG Amsterdam
Tel: +31 6 18054465
Page 69

Wild Wood
79 Kennington Road
Oxford
OX1 5PB
Tel: +44 7711 573 750
www.wildwood.ukwebz.com
*Pages 1, 16-31, 59, 60, 63 bottom, 64 right,
65 bottom right, 66 bottom, 67 top left*

With thanks to Tim Widdowson
for the illustrations on:
Pages 54, 55, 71, 78, 79